strange & beautiful people

Grey Gardner

BookLeaf
Publishing

India | USA | UK

Presentation by *BookLeaf Publishing*

Web: www.bookleafpub.com

E-mail: info@bookleafpub.com

ISBN: 9789358316315

First edition 2023

ACKNOWLEDGEMENT

Thank you to the Okanagan Freak Alliance for platforming me and telling the whole world what it means to carve out your place in it, and to my friends, who are my most loyal readers and supporters.

PREFACE

For me, the transgender thing is the reality of my life. It's the reality of my existence and it's something that I've come to believe is beautiful about me.

— Laverne Cox

the world

my heart is blown glass,
delicate and feather light
I am cautious in your palms
hollow, thin and
taunted by the silent swelling drop
to certain end beneath us
your warmth is an anchor
a weight while suspended in the air
without being in your hands I am not home,
empty nest that it would be without me
is there any way for Atlas
to rest his weary figure?
let me go for a moment
give a break to his shoulders
I gave you so many earths to bear
it would be okay to rest
if I don't get the chance to apologize
I wish you all the best

not sure what this poem was about

I don't have to try to forget you
it's so easy, in fact
there are days that trickle by
like racing raindrops
on a window pane,
they are all forgotten,
in a gutter someplace
and that was all natural

It's a simple task to forget you
one which requires no thought,
I don't remember any scars you showed me,
certainly not catching your eye,
nor do I remember your singing voice,
heavenly layered atop music
that has appeared on my CDs for no reason
tracks recommended by nobody,
a mystery, in fact

I have forgotten every story you told,
just like every dream I've had upon waking,
and every promise you made,
it was easy to forget,
after all I've made many promises to myself

that I'm sure I can't recall

it's easy to forget you,
I just have to remind myself
from time to time

genderqueer love affair

loving feels like living our truth,
perfect prisms shining through you
our bodies are just souls in one
we're drops of rain come together
drawn from the same cloud

perfect harmonies you sing with me,
our love alive with sound
aligned on a window pane
gender ebbs and flows away
only we remain,
foundations that built us fall away
like paint on a cottage door

you are meant to be mine,
as easily as the stars align
you are beautiful in your queer way
I am blessed by you in mine

touch me tenderly dear,
you make my pain less
my fears quiet and still
loving you is a dream
kissing you is heaven
touching you is sacred
I'm so glad we made it

lovers in the war (resistance)

the lover holds a picture
sooty thumb and forefinger
pinch the edges with gentleness
but hands tremble with hunger
exceedingly worsened with time,

breathe

the lover is alive,
breath short but steady,
is this what their last moment is like?
they can't take their eyes off of him
kindest smile in the world
feels as though they let him down
by their story not being told

breathe

the lover is alive,
they want to be free,
'if that were possible
how come they were taken from me?'

breathe

the lover regrets everything
it won't get any easier
it seems the only option to die
rather than ever look in another mirror

breathe

they wish they could apologize,
while they lay here and die,
in another time

silence

me myself and her

if it were possible to be two people
I'd be a woman
perhaps bi weekly
maybe by month.

sometimes I see her in VHS tapes
in pictures, cassettes
in a way she's beautiful,
a thing I've never considered
her face is lovely
her body delicate and sweet
in the mirror I am marked and plain,
without my makeup
I can't be sure what remains,

I'm a portrait of myself
if I were to have drawn it inverted

sometimes when I sleep,
she visits me in my mind
I don't think I'm pretty,
but she is kind

man-made earth

oil slicked parking lot,
slivered by vivid paint
cut in pieces by people
who don't remember the work,
wheels and shuffling feet
create rings of decomposition,
circling the sewage drain
in the nighttime it is empty,
corporate wasteland,
marred by bright blue and yellow stars
which don't exist upon asphalt
which don't shine in LED
I cry upon a curb,
while the flowers that have sprouted in the
sidewalk
tilt their heads in concern
all alone at Wal-Mart
all alone at home

comrade (amanda)

I love the way she turns bright
at the sight of a cat on the street
all creatures are her friends,
all people are her home

I love her fierce capacity,
to carve out a place for her type of person,
inviting people in like I,
wallflower experts and flies on the wall
we're under her umbrella in the rain
hand in hand with her at the climate rally
empowered words with her at the queer bar
I am writing on napkins.

I feel alien next to her, so human,
an example of something so honest and true
is hard to believe at all

she thinks my insect wings are beautiful,
she's not shy about celebrating
I used to feel hideous
but she makes me want to fly

archived online forum confession

to: editor@laqueerjournal.org
from: shygirl1990@hotmail.com
subject: re: the ordeal of existing
date: [corrupted data removed]

there were days
I wished I weren't gay
just as I'm sure
I'd wake up hoping for a
clean face,
no body aches
it would be easier
a convenient truth
to compress myself for a man
to distort myself for you
those days I wished away the transness
turned myself into a cis apologist
I wished I weren't gay
who wouldn't,
after every glaring look
every warning glance,
each threat to punish me and
my girlfriend for simply holding hands?
it is easiest to be straight

the hardest thing in the world to be something
everyone else hates

her profile picture is her face

for as long as I can remember
my friend Angel has no face,
she posts from time to time
about having seen herself during better days
judging harshly her features
dehumanizing her reflection
my friend Angel is honestly pretty,
captivating and softly feminine,
fierce and intimidating
my friend Angel has no face,
until one day she spends the night
soaking in the lights at her punk show,
blue and hazy,
a real lady
screaming freedom to a mic
swimming in her audience,
penning lyrics with her friends.
Angel is perfectly framed,
and one day I notice her picture has changed,
each angle of her smile cut from diamonds,
her shining soul on stage

red hourglass

neon signs cast ripples in the road
framed by cement pillars
at the outdoor parkade
the spiders have crawled out from
under my exhaust pipe
the yawning cobwebs reluctant to go
having made the hood of my car their own
only the drone of a clock radio
keeps me from my loneliness
it's useful to know what streets to take
and how to stop at a stoplight
may I trade this skill to write
to send a message to the world,
to you
it would be kinder to myself
if I could forget how to get home
just to stay with you
or touch your hands again

hunter's knife

I am ashamed of turning twenty five,
having spent so many years alive
drained by my own emptiness,
breaking my fingernails scraping my insides
for anything I can monetize
my age is a death sentence,
a slice of birthday cake
an unfair dreadful present of
human mortality
was I anyone past nineteen?
when will death catch up with me?
should I be scared and sow seeds of fear now
for when the reaper comes with his scythe
for the fresh bounty of hysteria
unresolvable grief?
If I were worthy of gentleness I would ask for it,
but I am sure all death is the same
just as I'm sure I won't have been done living
by the time I'm made to die

shadow flicker

the windmill is just
acting in routine,
warmed by the sun
and with shame it casts
shadow upon the valley
every rotation,
day after day
when it rains,
its blades are mirrors
the lighthouse can see itself from the bluff,
shining in warm yellow
a beloved beacon,
familiar figure
Windmill is empty, silo abandoned,
grain no longer needed in the empty valley,
no people to nourish with water or bread
but Lighthouse is still useful
even to those on land
more than anything
Windmill would like to be admired,
object of keychains and souvenirs
beloved by sailors too
but with no warm glow,
Windmill is a grey long shadow
and its blades take no breaks

a melancholic dance
a meaning without an end

totality complex

I miss the sun for a moment
as the moon takes the stage,
setting a curtain down
in its totality,
quicksilver dread
rests on every surface of my skin,
suddenly I am confronting the fear
of a sun's sudden absence

in the seconds the sun is draped by blue,
everything stops
and I am but a person on a cement block,
perhaps meaning nothing at all
in these seconds I am ironically eclipsed
by the greatness of the moon and sun
conducting their relationship in this way
in which I cannot understand
and could never replicate

capital ghoul

there are lineups of figures in not quite heaven
or hell
waiting for something that isn't coming
making money that isn't paper
to spend on goods they cannot eat

cashiers are blankly faced
as they are in this old life I lived,
and I cannot recall the last time I was asked
to give something other than pocket change
or receive anything but guilt in return

the ghosts next to me are shades of pale grey
filed in barcode lines with shadows
this earth has been hell quite like this
empty skull cases and uncaring stares
perfect assembly lines with no autonomy
not a single soul out of order at checkout

if death is the continuation of capital
I fear it more than the fade to black ending
and fear it more than the absence of sound

mine mine mine

embroidery shears
and hot glue,
DIY and home-brew
why buy paradise
we just make it our home
i want to die right where i was born
its a lot like drawing a circle
and connecting the ends
why live life if its not mine
I'm my own fuckin god
all knowing and divine
I've always chased tail
learned its my own,
bite down harder
as its all I've ever known
self fucking made,
self fulfilling prophecy
I own that
I know it

certain of you

you're just what I need
feel like I'll fit you perfectly
I want to be your missing piece
tangled legs under the sheets
summer lover born again
I'll do whatever it takes til it ends
lunar eclipse in the face of your sun
I was made to love you
I never want to run

open door policy

my home is where queer roses grow
between rainbow bookends and polaroids,
sheltered by vines that look loved
with leaves green and prosperous

my body is only my body,
no longer tortured by wild roaming eyes
perceiving its every natural state
as something to be gendered
as something to be criticized,
to be slandered
I am singing in the shower

my chosen family are butterflies
they create poetry that soars.
no longer tortured by wild roaming eyes,
no longer threatened by the hunger
of literary predators

my friend writes trans allegory
without fear or shame
we've shown each other our scars
and played music
while we laid in bed
pretending we were

roots or moss,
discriminated by nobody

my home is where my soulmate
finds new ways to tell me they love me
I feel free
I feel me

disposable income

"pay me back later" the first time we met,
I covered our coffee and taxi home
we were strangers once
but you're hard to forget
text messages lining my phone
I teased you from time to time
between promise rings and poetry lines
twenty bucks? cover me,
I'll get it next time
I paid the bill on our last date
it's somewhere crumpled in a bin,
I don't even want it back,
an investment in a lost cause
forgotten like the debt

rat

there is no worse fate
than being on my knees
in a glue trap
it is humiliating
to be stared at while I starve
if time moved any faster
my ribs would appear in order
my flesh would rot in rhythm
with parasites and scavengers
signing their names on my bones
removing the proof of my life
under settled dust and foundational decay
my adhesive strips the right for
my carbon dating future friend
chemical envelopes me
leaves nothing to be investigated

vulnerability in the form of a
skirt

I walk home in my dress.
it dances around my knees,
I cleaned a stain out of it
yesterday
and it is raining
while my boots eat up the distance
between me and my home
like black wolves

I am
disgusting
and yet it dances
as though nothing's wrong

I walk home in my dress
I can't do anything right

I watch a version of me
loom in the pond
they're eyeing up how wrong I am.

I want to run
but I walk
home because I'm

yesterday I cleaned a stain out of it.
it is disgusting.
I am

it mocks me with its dancing
it is no longer raining
I cleaned a stain yesterday
it is dancing
nothing is wrong

sunset cigarette

I want to go outside and have a smoke
I can't tell you what made me that way,
as I've never had the curiosity or the care to
cradle a Marlboro between my knuckles
or place it between my lips, no less

so I sit out in the cool evening air,
without anything to hold in my fingers save for a
pen
on days I'm not typing
rested gently in my hand like an old-fashioned
cigar.

from time to time I sit in my car,
with the windows down
and rest my wrist partly outside,
as though the smoke needs somewhere to go
when it does not exist.

at this point, I have become familiar with the
sound of the sprinklers lighting up
and it occurs to me the lawn is not green of its
own accord
I take a drag of cool midnight air
and contemplate this fact

I think I'd like to feel my guts surrounded by tar
and chemical,
but smoking wastes lots of cash anyways,
and I don't have an ash tray anyways,
and this is a habit anyways,
(I kill a bug with my bare foot
I don't put on shoes for these excursions.)

at least people who have "smoke breaks"
open their door once in a while
and know how to breathe
even when it's bad for them.